D1785263

1 MONTH OF
FREE
READING

at

www.ForgottenBooks.com

By purchasing this book you are
eligible for one month membership to
ForgottenBooks.com, giving you
unlimited access to our entire
collection of over 1,000,000 titles via
our web site and mobile apps.

To claim your free month visit:

www.forgottenbooks.com/free918359

ISBN 978-0-266-97697-4
PIBN 10918359

Vol. XXIV, No. 4   April, 1932   Total No. 100

Alabama College

The State College for Women

BULLETIN

THE SUMMER SCHOOL

SUPPLEMENT A

Published Quarterly by
ALABAMA COLLEGE
Montevallo, Alabama

Entered as second-class mail matter at the post-office at Montevallo, Alabama

Board of Trustees

His Excellency, BENJAMIN M. MILLER, Governor of Alabama,
President, *Ex-Officio*

A. F. HARMAN
State Superintendent of Education, *Ex-Officio*

OTHER OFFICERS

LOUISE C. COLEMAN (Mrs.) ....House Director

LUELLA GRISSOM (Mrs.) ....Executive Secretary

PATTIE HANEY ....Assistant in Registrar's Office

MARY E. HARRIS (Mrs.) ....House Director

ROBERTA HAYS ....Assistant Librarian

VIRGINIA HENDRICK ....Assistant Registrar

ANNA IRVIN ....Food Supervisor

IBBIE JONES ....Assistant Food Supervisor

ANNIE MARY JONES-WILLIAMS ....Secretary Home Study Service

WALTER MAURICE JONES-WILLIAMS ....Electrician

ANNIE LAURIE KILLINGSWORTH ....Nurse

MATTIE LEE ....Bookkeeper

GEORGIE LEEPER ....Manager Supply Store

MARVIN MALLORY ....Secretary to President

SUSIE MARSHALL ....Secretary to Dean

RUBY MARTIN ....Secretary to Student Counselor

FLORA BELLE SURLES ....Publicity Secretary

DOROTHY SUTER ....Assistant Librarian

OLLIE TILLMAN ....Nurse

NELLE WALKER ....Secretary School of Education

ALABAMA COLLEGE

O. Č. CARMICHAEL, M.A., B.Sc. (Oxon), LL.D., President

T. H. NAPIER, M.A., Ph.D., Dean
Director

M. L. ORR, M.A., Ph.D.
Assistant Director

FACULTY

A. C. ANDERSON --Education
B.A., Howard College. M.A., Teachers College, Columbia University.
Teacher and principal of rural schools; ten years county high school principal; County Superintendent of Education, Barbour County; Supervising Principal, Montgomery County Schools; President Newton Institute; Superintendent of Schools, Ozark, Alabama. Four years, Alabama College.

J. L. APPLETON --Training School
B.S., University of Alabama. Geraldine High School, one year; Alabama College Summer School, four summers. Alabama College Training School, six years.

MINNA McLEOD BECK ---Art
B.S., Columbia University. M.A., Columbia University. Salem College, North Carolina; University of Kentucky; Art Director, Harrisburg Public School; summer courses at University of Pittsburgh, University of Kentucky, University of North Carolina, Duke University, Western Reserve University; study and travel abroad summer of 1923. Four years, Alabama College.

VIRGINIA LEE BENNETT --------------------------------------Sociology
B.A., University of Louisville, Kentucky. Diploma from New York School of Social Work. Member of Alabama College Summer School faculty of 1929. One year, Alabama College.

ALICE BOYD --Education
B.S., George Peabody College for Teachers. M.A., Columbia University. Eight years in rural school supervision. Nine years, Alabama College.

MYRTLE BROOKE ---Sociology
B.A., George Peabody College for Teachers. M.A., Columbia University. Special study at University of Chicago and University of Tennessee. Six years, public schools of Georgia; four years of high school work in Louisiana. Twenty-one years at Alabama College.

P. H. CARMICHAEL --------------------------------Religious Education
B.S., University of Alabama. B.Ph., Mercer University. D.D., (Honorary) Southwestern University (Memphis). Ph.D., New York University. Certificate of Graduation, Princeton Theological Seminary. Instructor in University of Alabama Summer School. Ten years, Alabama College.

DURA-LOUISE COCKRELL ----------------------------Nursery School
B.A., Texas Christian University. M.A., Columbia University. Candidate for Ph.D. degree, Yale University. Two years, Kansas State Agricultural College. One year, Alabama College.

EDNA COLLINS ----------------------------------Progressive Education
Trained in Pratt Institute, New Jersey State Normal, and Teachers College, Columbia University. Experience in fourth and fifth grades, Passaic, New Jersey; art in junior high school, Elizabeth, New Jersey; fourth and fifth grades in the Tower Hill School, Wilmington, Delaware.

LEAH DENNIS _____English
>B.A., Northwestern University. M.A., Northwestern University. Ph.D. Stanford University. Southern College, Petersburg, Va., one year; St. Mary's School, Raleigh, N. C., two years; DePauw University, Greencastle, Ind., one year; El Paso Junior College, El Paso, Texas, six years. Alabama College, five years.

EUGENIA ECKFORD _____Art
>B.A., Mississippi State College for Women. M.A., Columbia University. Experience in North Carolina College for Women, Maryland State Normal School, University of North Carolina, visiting instructor at George Washington University, and the Tower Hill School, Wilmington, Delaware.

JOSEPHINE EDDY _____Home Economics
>B.S., M.A., Columbia University. Two summers abroad. Indianapolis Public Schools; State Clothing Specialist Alabama Extension Service; two summers Indiana University. Four years Alabama College.

MARGARET M. EDWARDS _____Home Economics
>B.S., Montana State College. M.A., Columbia University. Graduate work Chicago University, Cornell University. Assistant Professor of Home Economics, Florida State College for Women; Associate Professor of Education, Kansas State Agricultural College; State Supervisor of Home Economics Education, North Carolina; Staff Member of the American Child Health Association; Fellow, Laura Spelman Rockefeller Foundation. Professor of Home Economics, Alabama College, two years.

HALLIE FARMER _____History
>B.A., Indiana State Normal School. M.A., University of Wisconsin. Ph.D., University of Wisconsin. Teaching experience in high schools; Indiana State Normal School; teaching assistant, University of Wisconsin. Professor of History, Alabama College, five years.

KATHERINE FARRAH _____Voice
>B.A., University of Alabama. Artist's Diploma in Voice, University of Michigan. Study and travel in Europe. Marshall, Michigan, high school, one year; Stephens College, Missouri, five years. Alabama College, three years.

DORA GARRETT _____Biology
>B.A., Baylor University, Texas. Two years of graduate work at University of Wisconsin. Five years in public schools. Five years, Alabama College.

ELLEN-HAVEN GOULD _____Speech
>B.A., Coe College. Graduate School of Speech, Northwestern University. M.A., University of California. Student of School of Theatre, California. Player in Literary Theatre, Los Angeles. Coe College, four years; Washington State, two years; Occidental, one year. Alabama College, seven years.

LUELLA GRISSOM _____Secretarial
>B.A., Clinton College. Graduate Bowling Green Business University. Commercial experience; a number of years in office practice; training students in office practice; Blue Mountain College; commercial department, Athens College. Assistant instructor commercial department, Alabama College, five years.

RONALD INGALLS _____Violin
>B.M., Yale University School of Music. Private study with Loeffler and Becker. Teaching experience in Winston-Salem, N. C., City Schools; Illinois Woman's College; Baker University. One year, Alabama College.

FRANCES DOSS JACKSON _____Training School
>Attended Alabama College, Birmingham-Southern College and Howard College. Member of faculty of Alabama College Training School, three years.

ROSA LEA JACKSON _____Mathematics
>B.A., Western College. M.A., Ph.D., University of Chicago. Experience in Athens College, Alabama; Central College, Missouri; Ripley High School, Ripley, Tennessee; Northwestern University, Illinois; Leland Stanford Junior University; Hunter College of the City of New York. One year, Alabama College.

H. W. JAMES _____Education

B.S., Kansas State Teachers' College. Ph.D., University of Iowa. Six years public school work; Director Visual Service, University of Iowa; two summers special lecturer in education, University of Pittsburgh. Director School of Education of Alabama College since 1923.

W. J. KENNERLY _____Chemistry

B.S., Clemson College. M.S., Emory University. One year Assistant Professor of Chemistry at Clemson College. Alabama College, eleven years.

BESS B. LANE _____Progressive Education

Seven years of college and university education at Ypsilanti Normal College and the University of Michigan. Three years of travel and study in France and Germany. Four years, Director of Elementary Department, Tower Hill School, Wilmington, Delaware.

OLIVIA LAWSON _____Education

B.S., George Peabody College for Teachers. M.A., Teachers' College, Columbia University. Teaching experience in public schools of Alabama three years. Troy Normal School, one year; Supervisor of Schools, Walker County, four years. Alabama college, six years.

HARRISON D. LEBARON _____Music

B.A., Harvard University. M.A., Cornell University. Teacher and soloist New England Conservatory; American Guild of Organists; nine years Associate Professor of Music, Western College, Oxford, Ohio; two years Director of Music, Adrian College, Michigan; nine years, Ohio Wesleyan College, Delaware, Ohio. Director School of Music at Alabama College, two years.

ELSIE MAHAFFEY _____Physical Education

B.S., Alabama College. Teaching experience, Handley High School at Roanoke, Alabama; Citrus County High School, Florida; Instructor of Physical Education, Alabama College Summer School; Health and Physical Education teacher at Selma, Alabama, Junior High School; Counselor at National Girl Scout Camp, New York.

MARY E. McWILLIAMS _____History

B.S., Teachers' College, Columbia University. M.A., Columbia University. Instructor in piano, Alabama College, Pine Hill and Elmore County High Schools; Principal, Perdue Hill, Alabama; instructor in history and science, Pine Level and Pike Road High Schools. Instructor in History, Alabama College, six years.

MARIE HACKL MEANS _____Psychology

M.A., University of Kansas. Ph.D., Peabody College for Teachers. Teaching Fellowship, University of Kansas; Head Department of English, Gonzales High School, Texas; Normal Training Department, Parsons, West Virginia; Instructor of Education, Davis & Elkins College. Psychology, Alabama College, five years.

ELOISE MERONEY _____English

B.A., University of Alabama. M.A., Columbia University. Diploma, Alabama College. Further study Chicago University and Columbia University. Teacher of English, Chowan College, Ward-Belmont School, Judson College. Two years, Alabama College.

ALFREDA MOSSCROP _____Physical Education

B.A., Vassar College. M.A., University of Wisconsin. Certificate of Department of Hygiene, Wellesley College. Instructor in Woman's College of Delaware, Wellesley College, University of Wisconsin, Mary C. Wheeler School. Alabama College, two years.

MILTON LEE ORR _____Education

B.S., University of Alabama. M.A., George Peabody College for Teachers. Ph.D., George Peabody College for Teachers. Twelve years' experience in public schools; Superintendent of Alabama College Training Schools. Alabama College since 1922.

LORRAINE PETER _____History

B.A., Ripon College (Wisconsin). M.A., Columbia University. Warsaw High School (Wisconsin), three years; Beliot High School (Wisconsin), one year; Loulie Compton Seminary, Birmingham, Alabama, four years. Seven years, Alabama College.

CHARLOTTE PETERSON _____Training School

Diploma, Alabama College. Special study, Northwestern University, National Kindergarten and Elementary College. Twelve years in public schools. Seven years, Alabama College Training School.

ELIZABETH W. PFAUTZ _____Home Economics

B.S., M.S., Iowa State College. Instructor in Iowa State College, one year. Two years, Alabama College.

LORRAINE PIERSON _____Modern Languages

B.A., M.A., Transylvania College. M.A., University of Chicago. Degree Superieur, University of Dijon, Dijon, France. Ph.D., University of Illinois. Teaching experience in McKendree College, Lebanon, Illinois; University of Illinois. Four years, Alabama College.

COLIN B. RICHMOND _____Organ

Graduate New England Conservatory. Special student Harvard University. Graduate student New England Conservatory. Private study in theory with Elson and Mason. Organ with Goodrich and Dunham. Piano with Denee, Watson and Sequeria. Conducting and Composition with Chadwick and Converse. Public School Music and Methods study one year in England. One year Director of Music and Choir Master, St. Marks Church, Augusta, Maine; one year Director of Music and Sub-Master, Deerfield Academy, Deerfield, Massachusetts; five years Director of Music, Tennessee Polytechnic Institute; one year Examiner and Director of Music, Boston Council of Girl Scouts; one year, Pennsylvania State College. Seven years, Alabama College.

ELSA SCHNEIDER _____Physical Education

B.A., University of Wisconsin. Diploma, Chicago Normal College. Four years in high schools of Illinois; summer school University of Wisconsin; one year substitute instructor, Chicago Y. W. C. A. One year, Alabama College.

CLEVELAND G. SHARP _____Biology

B.S., M.S., Alabama Polytechnic Institute. Candidate for the doctorate at University of Chicago. Four years of teaching experience in high schools. Eleven years, Alabama College.

MARTHA SHOVER _____Library Science

B.A., M.A., Oglethorpe University, Georgia. Certificate in Library Science, Emory University, Georgia. Graduate work, Chicago University. Experience in High Point, N. C., High School; Library School, Carnegie Library of Atlanta, Ga.; Asheville, N. C., Normal & Associated Schools; Asheville, N. C., Senior High School; Carnegie Library of Atlanta; State Library, Atlanta. Alabama College, one year and one summer school.

MINNIE L. STECKEL _____Education

B.A., University of Kansas. M.A., University of Chicago. Ph.D., University of Chicago. Principal high school, ten years. Superintendent of Public Schools, two years. North Dakota State Teachers' College, one year. Public School Psychologist, two years. Student Counselor, Alabama College, two years.

J. R. STEELMAN _____Sociology

B.A., Henderson-Brown College. M.A., Vanderbilt University. B.D., and Ph.D., University of North Carolina. Teaching Fellow and Assistant in Department of Sociology, Vanderbilt University; Assistant, Economics, Harvard Summer School; Professor of Sociology and Economics, Hampton Institute, Virginia, summer school. Four years, Alabama College.

ESTER STEWART _____Progressive Education

Attended Cleveland School of Art; College of William and Mary; Western Reserve University—Department of Nursery, Kindergarten, Primary Education (graduated). Experience in Louise Rawson Day Nursery, Cleveland, Ohio; Nursery Play School, Cleveland; Country Day School, Mansfield, Ohio; The Park School, Cleveland; Tower Hill School, Wilmington, Delaware.

ELIZABETH STOCKTON _____Modern Language

B.S., M.A., University of Missouri. Foreign study in National University of Mexico and study and travel in Europe. Stephens College, Missouri, seven years. Alabama College, four years.

ALICE STRIBLING --Home Economics

B.A., Winthrop College. M.S., University of Tennessee. High School teacher; Itinerant Teacher Trainer, Alabama College. Assistant Professor of Home Economics, Alabama College, two years.

BLANCHE TANSIL ---Home Economics

B.S., University of Tennessee. M.A., George Peabody College for Teachers. Four years, Southwest Texas Teachers College; three years, George Peabody College for Teachers; one year, University of Kentucky; two years, Alabama College.

ARTHUR W. VAUGHAN --English

B.S., Central College. M.A., Harvard University. Ph.D., George Peabody College for Teachers. Austin scholar in English at Harvard University; instructor in English, Central College Academy and Marvin Junior College; Educational Director of the Ralph Sellew Institute; Head of the Department of English and Public Speaking, Southeast Missouri State Teachers' College. Four years, Alabama College.

KATHERINE VICKERY --------------------------------------Psychology

B.A., North Georgia Agricultural College. M.A., and Ph.D., George Peabody College for Teachers. Teacher in high schools three years. Alabama College since 1922.

J. S. WARD --Modern Language

B.A., Howard College. M.A., University of Alabama. Graduate student, University of Chicago. M.A., Columbia University. Candidate for the doctorate, Columbia University. Experience in public school system as principal and superintendent; two years, Baylor University; one year, Howard Payne College; one year, Mercer University; five years, A. & M., of Texas; one year as German Instructor, Columbia University; one year, University of Alabama; Director of Summer School and Acting Dean, Alabama College, 1924; Instructor of German, Summer School, Columbia University, 1927. Nine years, Alabama College.

SADIE WEIR ---Training School

B.S., M.A., George Peabody College for Teachers. Five years public school work; eight years high school work. Five years, Alabama College.

LILLIAN WORLEY ---History

B.A., Alabama College. One year Instructor in History, Alabama College.

MARY WRIGHT --Nursery School

B.S., Alabama College. One year Assistant in the Nursery School, Alabama College.

MARY V. ZIELINSKI ---------------------------------Public School Music

B.M.E., Northwestern University. Twelve years teacher and supervisor of music in public schools of Michigan. Alabama College, three years.

MIECISLAW ZIOLKOWSKI --------------------------------------Piano

Graduate of Stern Conservatory, Berlin, Germany. Master Class at Stern Conservatory. Switzerland with Paderewski. Teacher in Stern Conservatory, two years; Warsaw Conservatory, two years; Columbia School of Music, Chicago, three years. Alabama College, three years.

Foreword

The seventeenth Summer School at Alabama College will begin June 9, 1932. The first term will end July 16. The second term will begin July 18 and end August 20. The two terms are each separate units, so that students may pursue work for either term or for the full summer quarter. In the latter event, twelve semester hours of credit may be earned. Students having a "B" average may take a maximum of fourteen semester hours during the summer school.

The attention of students is called to the fact that Alabama College is a standard institution, being a member of the Association of Alabama Colleges, the Association of Colleges and Secondary Schools of the Southern States, and the Association of American Colleges, and granting degrees in the regular academic subjects, music, home economics, art, physical education, secretarial science, sociology and social service. The cost of attending Alabama College is reasonable in comparison with that of other institutions of equal standing.

Alabama College is fortunately situated to offer the students and teachers of the state a summer school meeting adequately their needs for both pleasure and profit. On the succeeding pages are offered for consideration a number of advantages which may be enjoyed by those who will come to the Summer School.

ADVANTAGES OF ALABAMA COLLEGE SUMMER SCHOOL

General

I. During the Summer School at Alabama College a student may complete one-third of a full session's work. Many members of the regular faculty teach throughout the summer term. Students are encouraged to pursue college courses for credit toward a degree. These college credit courses enable the student to:

A. Graduate in three years if she completes the normal amount of work in the three summer schools.

B. Remove conditions or make up back-work.

C. Advance culturally. Those who are interested in their own cultural progress will find a fruitful field in the courses offered in the various departments of the college.

II. Montevallo is ideally located in the center of the state. The altitude is high, the climate healthful and the campus, which includes ninety-six acres of ground, affords ample facilities for recreation. There are tennis courts, basket-ball courts, hockey, volley ball, and hand ball courts, and a large swimming pool. Special swimming lessons are given at a reasonable rate.

III. The dormitories are large, well ventilated, well screened, have electric lights, hot and cold water, and are well equipped to care for those who come.

IV. The food and dining room service are excellent. A trained dietitian who provides a good, wholesome, well-prepared and well-balanced ration is in charge of the dining room.

Curriculum

Courses are offered in Art, Biology, Chemistry and Physics, Education, English, History, Home Economics, Library Science, Mathematics, Modern Languages, Music, Physical Education, Psychology, Religious Education, Typewriting, Sociology, and Speech.

The courses are so arranged that students may complete a year's work in such fundamental courses as Biology, Chemistry, English, History, Mathematics, and Modern Languages, by remaining for the entire eleven weeks.

In the other departments many of the courses are so organized that a student may complete a full year's work in either six or eleven weeks. The work in Typewriting is offered to meet the needs of teachers, administrators, social workers, and students in general who are not taking the regular Secretarial course.

˙Special Features

PROGRESSIVE EDUCATION DEMONSTRATION SCHOOL AND INSTITUTE FOR ELEMENTARY SCHOOL TEACHERS, JUNE 9-JULY 16

ALABAMA COLLEGE SUMMER SCHOOL SELECTED

The Progressive Education Association will sponsor during the first six weeks of the 1932 Alabama College Summer School a Demonstration School and Institute of Progressive Education for the southeastern section of the United States.

NATURE OF WORK TO BE OFFERED

Owing to the fact that this will be the first Demonstration School and Institute sponsored by the Progressive Education Association in the South, it was deemed advisable to confine the work this year to the elementary school. However, a course in Materials and Methods as it applies to high school will be offered by the staff of the Alabama College School of Education.

The Elementary Training School will be in charge of a director and three demonstration teachers nominated by the Progressive Education Association and three of our regular Training School staff. The teachers representing the Progressive Education Association are:

Mrs. Bess B. Lane, Director
Miss Ester Stewart, Second Grade
Miss Edna Collins, Fifth Grade
Miss Eugenia Eckford, Art in the Grades

These people are experienced teachers in one of the leading progressive education schools of the country, the Tower Hill School of Wilmington, Delaware. A part of our regular Training School faculty will act as assistants and have charge of the First, Third, Fourth, and Sixth Grades.

The Demonstration School and Institute will serve the following classes of students:

1. Those who attend Summer School for the progressive education work alone. A full term's work carrying six semester hours of credit may be taken.
2. Those who desire to take one or two courses in progressive education and one or two courses in other fields.
3. Those who desire to spend a few days without credit observing the work in the Demonstration School. No tuition fee will be charged for those attending less than two weeks for this observation. Board will be furnished at reasonable rates.

In addition to the demonstration of progressive practice, the following courses ʻin progressive education, each carrying two semester hours of credit, will be given:

1. Materials and Methods for the Lower Elementary Grades
2. Materials and Methods for the Upper Elementary Grades

3. Directed Observation in the Lower Elementary Grades
4. Directed Observation in the Upper Elementary Grades
5. Materials and Methods for High School
6. Art as It Functions in the Lower Elementary Grades
7. Art as It Functions in the Upper Elementary Grades

The above courses are outlined under the description of education courses as Education S303, S370, S381, S382, S391, and S392, on page 24.

Those interested in progressive education materials and methods for the pre-school age child may enroll in Home Economics 400, The Nursery School.

PROGRESSIVE EDUCATION

Progressive education is a world-wide movement. It is not a panacea, rejecting accepted beliefs, adult judgments and traditions. Rather, it is a new approach to the study of the child, a belief that the development of his normal interests exceeds in importance the imposing of standardized subject matter. It assumes that education develops from human experiences, rather than results from the acquisition of information and the cultivation of skills for deferred needs. It is liberal and humanitarian rather than compelling and mechanistic.

The Progressive Education Association was founded in 1919 for the dissemination of progressive education theory and practice. It includes among its officers and directors such outstanding educators as Dr. John Dewey, Dr. William H. Kilpatrick, and Dr. Harold Rugg of Columbia University; Dr. William J. Cooper, United States Commissioner of Education; Miss Lucy Gage, of Peabody College; Mr. Charleton Washburn, of the Winnetka, Illinois, schools; and Miss Flora J. Cook, Principal of the Frances W. Parker School, of Chicago.

PREVIOUS DEMONSTRATION SCHOOLS AND INSTITUTES

Three years ago a summer Institute of Progressive Education was inaugurated by the Progressive Education Association at the Pennsylvania State College. During the summer of 1930 the Institute was held for six weeks at Vassar College. The third Institute was held for six weeks during the summer of 1931 at Syracuse University. A Demonstration School was added at this time.

PROGRESSIVE EDUCATION IN THE SOUTHEASTERN SECTION

While the Progressive Education Demonstration School and Institute to be held at Alabama College will be the first of its kind in the South, progressive education theory and practice are not new in this section. The first day of the Regional Conference of Supervisors held in Montgomery during December was devoted entirely to discussions of the progressive education movement. Progressive education is being stressed by state and county supervisors in a number of the southern states. An examination of the new Alabama Elementary Course of Study will reveal the extensive use of progressive education principles.

STATE DEPARTMENT OF EDUCATION APPROVES

The Progressive Education Demonstration School and Institute to be held during the first six weeks of the Alabama College Summer School has the hearty approval of the Alabama State Department of Education and is especially endorsed by the Division of Teacher Training and Elementary Education.

SCHOOL OF MUSIC—JUNE 9-JULY 16

The School of Music of Alabama College offers a number of special features for the summer school of 1932 as well as the regular work leading to the Bachelor of Music degree.

A group of courses has been organized which will serve those who are already established musicians and wish to add to their repertory or to re-study and re-interpret familiar works. To permit full consideration of more extended compositions two one-hour lessons a week are assigned in this group of courses. The lessons are private and it will be possible to register in these courses for the entire six weeks or for a shorter length of time for those who cannot remain throughout the term. Registrations for the repertory courses include registration in the lecture class in piano and in organ and in the ensemble class for those taking violin.

The special work in organ is under the direction of Mr. C. B. Richmond and Mr. H. D. LeBaron. The piano instruction will be given by Mr. Miecislaw Ziolkowski. Mr. Ronald W. Ingalls will have charge of the work in violin, while Miss Katherine Farrah will give instruction in voice.

NURSERY SCHOOL—JUNE 9-JULY 16

The Nursery School will be in session during the first term of the summer school and may be used by students in home economics and in education for observing the interests and responses of little children in their various activities. The child development course may be taken as an integral part of the work sponsored by the Progressive Education Association by those interested in the pre-school age child.

SCHOOL OF INSTRUCTION—JUNE 1-JUNE 17

A three weeks' course is given for Alabama teachers of vocational home economics. The purpose of this unit is to give specific aid in organizing the year's program, in setting up standards and in applying modern methods of education to home economics instruction.

ALUMNAE INSTITUTE—JUNE 17-18

Believing that education should be projected beyond the four years spent in formal study on the campus in pursuit of a diploma or a degree, President Carmichael has arranged for an Alumnae Institute to be held on the campus, June 17-18. The program will provide general inspirational topics, and special subjects which should appeal to special groups. Children of Alumnae will be cared for during the program hours by the college Nursery School staff. Some outstanding leaders in the fields of special interest to women are being sought for the Institute program, and it is believed that many former students of the college will experience again the satisfaction which comes from a consciousness of intellectual growth and social fellowship among well-remembered scenes.

Further details may be had upon application to the alumnae office at the college, or to the Chairman of the Program Committee, Miss Myrtle Brooke.

FIRST ANNUAL INSTITUTE OF DEANS OF WOMEN AND ADVISERS TO GIRLS, JUNE 27-JULY 1

Feeling the need for more knowledge and a better understanding of the modern adolescent girl, the Alabama Association of Deans of Women and Advisers to Girls at their annual meeting in Birmingham in March voted unanimously to hold their First Annual Institute at Alabama College from June 27 to July 1, inclusive.

The plans for the program provide for courses by outstanding members of the Alabama College faculty and by other prominent educators in the State. A member of the National Staff of Girl Scouts will conduct a Girl Scout Leadership Course and will give Scout Leadership Certificates to those completing the course successfully.

The courses offered will include series of lectures on: Personality and Human Adjustment, Diagnostic and Remedial Teaching, Vocational Guidance, The Physical Education Program for the Adolescent Girl, Religious Issues of the Machine Age, Guiding and Training the Adolescent Girl through the Home Economic Program, and Administration of the High School Girl. In addition to these lectures there will be round table discussion on current educational problems in which many of the educators of the State will participate.

There will be no fee for instruction. The cost for board and room will be $5.00 for the Institute period.

The Progressive Education Institute will be in session at this time and meetings will be open to visitors. Each evening there will be a recreational period and entertainment of music and dramatics. The tennis courts and swimming pool will be at the disposal of the women attending this Institute.

This Institute is especially for Girl Advisers but is open to any high school teacher interested in the adolescent girl. Ramsay Hall, the Senior Dormitory, will be headquarters for the Institute.

For further information regarding the Institute, address Olive Stone, President of the Association, Woman's College, Montgomery, Alabama, or Minnie L. Steckel, Secretary, Montevallo, Alabama.

GIRLS' CAMP AT ALABAMA COLLEGE

July 18-July 31
August 1-August 15

This camp will be for girls from ages 10 to 16 years; for Girl Scouts and all girls interested in camping. The camp will include hiking, swimming, tennis, archery, nature lore, camp craft, sketching, basketry, clay modeling, pageantry, dramatics, folk dancing, and other activities which make for fun and happiness.

For particulars write to Minnie L. Steckel, Student Counselor, Alabama College, who will be Camp Director.

SYNODICAL TRAINING SCHOOL—JUNE 22-JUNE 28

The Synodical Training School of the Presbyterian Church, which has held its meetings for the past two years at Woman's College, Montgomery, Alabama, will meet this year at Alabama College, June 22 to June 28.

ALABAMA WRITERS' CONCLAVE—JUNE 13-16

The Alabama Writers' Conclave will hold its annual session at Alabama College from June 13 to June 16. Their programs are open to the public and may be shared in by the members of the Summer School. In addition to that, special speakers who will come for the Conclave will be available for lectures to the Summer School.

ENTERTAINMENT FEATURES

The College plans an enlarged program of recreation and entertainment during both terms of the Summer School. These include among other features:

1. Music and speech recitals by members of the faculty.
2. Plays and stunts put on by students.
3. Visiting lecturers and entertainers.
4. Educational pictures.
5. Clock Golf, Quoits, Tennis, Croquet, Basketball, Volley Ball, Indoor Baseball, and other games.
6. Athletic tournaments of various kinds.
7. Hikes and camp suppers.
8. Evening play hour under the direction of a playground supervisor.
9. Camphouse and Swimming Pool open free of charge to students.
10. Annual picnic at the Camphouse.
11. Evening group-singing hour under the direction of a song leader.
12. Reception given to summer school students by the faculty.
13. Excursions organized to points of interest in Alabama.
14. Other features to be announced later.

Equipment

The entire equipment of Alabama College is used by the Summer School students. This includes three splendidly equipped dormitories for eight hundred pupils, an infirmary, a library, a new auditorium and administration building, a music building, two classroom buildings, two training school buildings, a home management house, the college laundry, the dairy, the gymnasium, the swimming pool and other athletic equipment.

The library will be open from 8:00 A. M. to 9:00 P. M., daily.

Students may purchase stationery, tablets, college text books, and other needed equipment at the supply store. High school students should secure the state-adopted text books from some local depository.

GENERAL INFORMATION

The Summer School was established in May, 1915, by order of the Board of Trustees and held its first session in 1916. A six or twelve weeks' session has been held every summer since that time. The session of 1932 will be eleven weeks in length, beginning June 9 and ending August 20. The first term will be six weeks in length, with class work on alternate Saturdays, and it will begin June 9 and end July 16. The second term will be five weeks in length, six days a week, beginning July 18 and ending August 20. The work of each term will be a unit in itself and students who attend only one term may secure full credit for all work completed.

The aim of the Alabama College Summer School is to serve in the fullest way the interest of public education in the state. Special attention is given to the following:

1. Those who wish to obtain, renew, or extend certificates.

2. High school teachers and others who do not hold college degrees but wish to obtain credit toward their degrees.

3. Public school teachers who wish to study methods of teaching any grade of school work.

4. Alabama College students, and those from other colleges, who wish to remove conditions by summer work.

5. Those who desire special work in Home Economics, Music, Art, Speech, Physical Education, or other special fields.

6. Home Economics teachers who desire to teach in the junior and senior high schools or to increase their knowledge of the subject.

7. Those who wish to take regular home economics courses.

8. Those who wish a thorough course in public school music, or who wish to prepare for the state examination in piano or public school music.

9. Those who wish to take general physical education courses to prepare to teach physical education in the schools or to coach basket ball or other games.

10. Those who are interested in master classes in violin, piano, and organ.
11. Those who are interested in library science.
12. Those who wish to secure high school credit.

EXPENSES FOR FIRST TERM

Room, board and laundry $36.00
Matriculation fee 3.00
Physician, nurse, hospital and medicine fee 1.00
Fee for 6 semester hours of work 12.00

    Total $52.00

EXPENSES FOR SECOND TERM

Room, board and laundry $30.00
Physician, nurse, hospital and medicine 1.00
Fee for 6 semester hours of work 12.00

    Total $43.00

A fee of $2.00 per semester hour is charged for college courses taken for credit. Any student, therefore, who takes more than 6 semester hours per term will pay $2.00 for each additional hour of credit taken.

A student who was not in attendance during the first term will pay the matriculation fee of $3.00 for the second term.

No reduction in price will be made to students who do not have their laundry done in the college laundry.

Parents entering children in the Nursery School for the first term will pay a fee of $5.00 for each child.

Students who take laboratory courses in Science will pay the fees indicated below:

Fees (Per Term)

Bacteriology $6.00
Biology 4.50
Chemistry 4.50
Physics 4.50
Clothing 2.00
Foods 5.00
Other Home Economics Courses (each) 2.00
Swimming Lessons (12) 2.00
Use of Typewriter 3.00

A fee of $4.00 per half-unit of credit is charged for high school courses.

(For music fees, see Music Department, page 33.)

Equipment

Each student should bring with her: 1 teaspoon, 1 glass, 1 pillow, 2 pillow cases, 2 bed spreads, 4 sheets (only single or three-quarter beds are used), blankets or comforts, umbrella, towels, 2 clothes bags, raincoat, overshoes.

COLLEGE AND HIGH SCHOOL CREDIT

High school and college students will have the privilege of studying to remove conditions or to secure advanced standing. As a rule, courses of study satisfactorily completed in the Summer School will be credited in the regular session, provided such studies form part of the regular course.

Those interested in high school courses see page 41.

REGISTRATION

Registration will take place Thursday, June 9. Students will be registered on later dates, but full credit of attendance may not be given for those entering after June 13. Class work will begin Friday, June 10, at 8:00 A. M. All students who have not registered and paid their fees by 12:00 o'clock, Friday, June 10, will pay the late registration fee of $2.00.

Students who pay the $2.00 room reservation fee and find that they are unable to attend the Summer School may have this fee refunded provided the Director of the Summer School is notified by June 1.

Students attending the Summer School who wish to board in the town of Montevallo should get the approval of the President, or the Director of the Summer School.

INTRODUCTION OF NEW COURSES

The officials of the Summer School reserve the right to introduce new courses in the place of those for which no students enroll when the demand for such courses justifies the introduction.

REDUCED RAILROAD RATES

The Southeastern Passenger Association has granted reduced rates on round trip tickets to the Alabama College Summer School from all points in Alabama. The round trip fare will be one and one-half fare, with a minimum excursion fare of $1.00. Tickets will be sold June 6 to June 13 inclusive, and July 14 to July 20 inclusive. The final limit of these tickets will be August 26, 1932. In order to secure this reduced rate it will be necessary for each student to have an identification certificate, which will be supplied by the Director of the Summer School upon request. This certificate should be presented to the local ticket agent by those desiring reduced railroad rates.

RENEWAL AND EXTENSION OF TEACHERS' CERTIFICATES

The regulations below are those approved by the State Department of Education and apply to the Alabama College Summer School for 1932.

Certificates issued on examination or by validation from other states may be renewed for one-half the period of their original life on six weeks of work. To count as six weeks of work a student must obtain a minimum of six semester hours. The above certificates may be reinstated for the full period of original validity on twelve weeks' work with twelve semester hours. This work should be in the field in which the certificate has been issued.

*Class B Elementary Certificates (issued prior to 1928) or other elementary certificates, based upon the completion of one year normal work, may be reinstated by taking the outlined course prescribed in the catalog for this purpose.

Class B Secondary Certificates (issued prior to 1928) or other secondary certificates, based upon three years of college work, may be reinstated by taking courses leading to the issuance of the certificate next higher in rank. Unless a class B secondary certificate has already been extended on an additional twelve weeks of study in a college or university, twelve weeks of study in residence with twelve semester hours of credit entered on the records will be required for its reinstatement.

Class A Elementary Professional, Class A Secondary Professional, and Special Subject certificates (issued prior to 1928) may be reinstated by taking courses for which credit toward graduation is allowed. No credit may be allowed toward the reinstatement of such certificates for a course shorter than six weeks for which the student receives at least six semester hours or nine quarter hours of credit.

*Subjects prescribed for the renewal of certificates which have been issued upon the basis of one year of college work:

American Literature	2 semester hours
American History	2 semester hours
Geography of Europe	2 semester hours
Teaching of Reading	2 semester hours
School Management	2 semester hours
Public School Music	1 semester hour
Drawing	1 semester hour
Physical Education	1 semester hour
Total	13

All students who want certificates issued, extended, continued or renewed should see Dr. H. W. James, Director of Education, immediately after they have been classified and fill out a form for the certificate desired. Holders of certificates to be continued, extended, or renewed should bring such certificates with them when they come to Alabama College, and should attach these to the form submitted to Dr. James.

COURSES OF STUDY

ART

The Art Department offers courses planned to suit the needs of the designer and creative artist, as well as training for the grade teacher who wishes to secure from her pupils original work of a high order.

The courses offered below may be supplemented by others concerned with more advanced work should there be a demand for them.

Art S111. **Art Structure.** An introductory course dealing with fundamental principles. Required of all students majoring in Art. Lecture and creative work. First and second terms. Credit, 3 semester hours each term.

Art S112. **Art Structure.** A continuation of Art S111. First and second terms. Credit, 3 semester hours each term.

Art S140. **Elementary Pottery.** Lectures and laboratory work. Art principles applied to pottery and modeling. Second term. Credit, 2 semester hours.

Art S150. **Related Art.** This course is given primarily for Home Economics students. It treats of art principles in relation to line, tone, and color. First and second terms. Credit, 3 semester hours each term.

Art S240. **Pottery.** Lecture and laboratory work. The principles of art as applied to shapes in the round. Work with clay built up forms, modeling, etc., soap sculpture, mask making, cement work, etc. Required of Art majors. Prerequisite: Art 251 or 140 and 111. Second term. Credit, 3 semester hours.

Art S251. **Art Structure.** A course dealing with the three elements of art, line, tone, and color, as affected by the various principles of balance, rhythm, subordination, etc. Prerequisite: Art 112. Required of all Art majors. Second term. Credit, 3 semester hours.

Art S300.1. **Public School Art.** Methods and subject matter lectures, creative work, and consideration of appropriate problems for each grade—elementary and high school. First term. Credit, 2 semester hours.

BIOLOGY

Biology S101. **Botany.** A general course dealing briefly with the four phyla of the plant kingdom; the cell, the function of cells, and cell division; the kind, structure and uses of the root, stem, leaves, buds, fruits, and seeds; and a study of such algae, fungi, liverworts, mosses, and ferns as time will permit. Three lectures and five two-hour laboratory periods a week. First term. Credit, 3 semester hours.

Biology S102 or S110. **Zoology.** Beginning with the Amoeba as representative of living protoplasm, and of the lowest group of animals, the various phyla are studied in their evolutionary sequence. Time does not permit of a study of all the groups, but such representatives as the following are examined: Amoeba, Paramecium, Euglena, Pandorina, Volvox, Hydra, Obelia, Gonionemus, Grantia, Planaria, Tapeworm, Ascaris, Earthworm, and the Frog. A study is also made of the great scientists in various fields of Biology, together with the contribution each has made. Three lectures and five two-hour laboratory periods a week. Second term. Credit, 3 semester hours.

Biology S210. **General Physiology and Hygiene.** This course is both practical and scientific as it treats of the structure and functions of the various organs of the body and means of maintaining them in health. Being a basic science it gives knowledge of the principles underlying Psychology, Physical Culture, Dietetics, and Hygiene. In addition, it is also designed to qualify the teachers of the elementary grades and high school for the intelligent direction of a systematic and effective health program in the home, school, and community. Lectures will be supplemented by demonstration work for the purpose of illustrating and simplifying many of the topics studied. Eight lectures a week. First term. Credit, 3 semester hours.

Biology S220. **Bacteriology.** This course will deal with the morphology, physiology, and cultivation of bacteria, yeast, and molds. Special consideration will be given to the relation of micro-organisms to the preservation, preparation, and handling of foods; to their relation to water and milk supply and sewage disposal; and to the organisms occasionally found in various foods, water and milk that cause disease. The course will be of such nature as is needed for students taking home economics and for those desiring to become acquainted with the fundamental principles of bacteriology and sanitation. One lecture and three two-hour laboratory periods a week. First and second terms. This course is continuous and must be taken both terms. Credit, 3 semester hours.

Biology S252. **Nature Study.** This course is designed for teachers and is required of all persons preparing to teach in elementary schools. Those who teach biology in high school will also be greatly helped by this course because it will furnish much valuable information of outdoor-life and give practice in finding, assembling and using this information in teaching. It consists of a study of both plants and animals in the field. Emphasis is placed on the study of birds, insects, local flora, and wild life in general. Studies in nature are demonstrated by assigned projects. Two lectures and four two-hour laboratory periods a week. First term. Credit, 2 semester hours.

Biology S310. **Bacteriology.** (Preventive Medicine, Parasitology, and Sanitation.) A general course dealing with the cause of the most common contagious, infectious, and non-infectious diseases, their importance, and how to prevent them. The laboratory will consist of a study of the common parasites of man and their relation to human diseases. Some other topics discussed will be milk, water, and sewage in relation to health and methods of bettering home, school, industrial, and city sanitation. Students may take the lecture work and omit the laboratory work, but will receive only 2 semester hours credit for so doing. Six lectures and three two-hour laboratory periods a week. Second term. Credit, 2 or 3 semester hours.

Note: If there is not sufficient demand some courses may not be offered the second term. It will be noted that a full year's work in Biology may be completed during the eleven weeks of summer school, thus satisfying the Science requirement for either the A.B. degree, or one year's work for those taking any course majoring in Science.

CHEMISTRY AND PHYSICS

Chemistry S101. **General Chemistry.** This course is identical with the first semester's work in General Chemistry as offered in the regular session. It consists of a study of the common elements. Laboratory experiments accompany the regular lecture work. First term. Credit, 3 semester hours.

Chemistry S102. **General Chemistry.** A continuation of course S101, embracing the second semester's work in General Chemistry. Second term. Credit, 3 semester hours.

Chemistry S211. **Quantitative Analysis.** This course embraces a study of those methods of analysis which are usually employed in determining the constituents of simple compounds. Gravimetric determinations are made in this course with stress being given to the importance of accurate laboratory manipulations. Credit, 3 semester hours.

Chemistry S212. **Quantitative Analysis.** This course is a continuation of S211. The work in this course deals with simple volumetric methods of analysis. Standard solutions are made by the student and volumetric determinations are made upon a number of compounds. Credit, 3 semester hours.

Chemistry S331, S332. **Organic Chemistry.** This course during the first semester deals with the fundamental principles of Organic Chemistry, special emphasis being given to fats, carbohydrates, and proteins. This is followed the second term by a course in Foods and Physiological Chemistry, dealing chiefly with the digestive action of saliva, gastric fluid, etc., on foods. Required of all regular Home Economics students. First and second terms. Credit, 3 semester hours each term.

Chemistry S353. **Physiological Chemistry.** Designed especially for Home Economics students. Only students who have had General Chemistry and Organic Chemistry will be admitted to this course. First term. Credit, 2 semester hours.

Physics S201. **General Physics.** A course in general physics involving a study of the systems of measurements, laws of machines, gravitation and electricity. Credit, 3 semester hours.

Physics S340. **Household Physics.** A semester's course for those students majoring in the Home Economics Department. The laboratory work in this course will consist of experiments on household appliances involving physical principles. Visits are made to the power house, ice plant and pump house in order to study how these plants utilize the physical principles discussed in the classroom. Credit, 3 semester hours.

EDUCATION

Education S300. **School Management.** This course deals with the general classroom problems of the elementary teacher, including discipline, school records, school hygiene, etc. First term. Credit, 2 semester hours.

Education S301. **Principles of High School Teaching.** This course takes up problems applicable to all high school teachers, such as discipline, class management, examinations, teachers' reports, and so forth. Required of all applicants for the College Secondary Class B Certificate, and all Special Certificates to teach in high school. Open to all juniors. First term. Credit, 3 semester hours.

Education S303. **Progressive Education in the High School.** This course will attempt an interpretation of Progressive Education to the high school teacher. It will also trace the development of the concept of Progressive Education from its sources. Some of the topics discussed in the course will be: the place of control in education, basic principles of a progressive school, the problem and the project, the appreciation concept, measurement and the new education, and socialization. (May be substituted for Education 302, for any directed elective, or for Education 490 for seniors.) First term. Credit, 3 semester hours.

Education S311. **Methods of Teaching Reading in the Lower Elementary Grades.** This course will deal primarily with the methods in the lower grades. However, a discussion of the reading in the upper grades will be included with less emphasis. Required of all students taking the four-year elementary curriculum preparing to teach in the lower elementary grades. First term. Credit, 2 semester hours.

Education S312. **Methods of Teaching Social Science in the Lower Elementary Grades.** This course will take up the entire field of social science in the first six grades. The project work in the lower grades will be given most emphasis. Required of all students taking the four-year elementary curriculum, preparing to teach in the lower grades. Second term. Credit, 2 semester hours.

Education S360. **Vocational Guidance Through Girls' Organizations.** The organization, aims, and methods of national organizations for girls; including Girl Reserves, Girl Scouts, and Camp Fire Girls will be considered with the purpose of preparing the prospective teacher or social worker for organizing and directing such groups in connection with school, church, or civic work. Elective. First term. Credit, 2 semester hours.

Education S370. **Directed Observation in the Elementary School.** This course is an introduction to directed teaching. There will be observation and discussion of the teaching of all of the elementary school subjects. First term. Credit, 2 semester hours.

Education S380. **Visual Education.** This course deals with the importance of visual education in teaching. Instruction will be given both in the source and in the use of visual materials. Special emphasis will be placed upon the technique of the use of pictures, stereoptican slides and motion pictures, as instruments of learning. Second term. Credit, 2 semester hours.

Education S381. **Philosophies, Materials and Methods in the Primary Grades.** In this course problems similar to the following will be considered: In what way has education changed? What has brought about this change? What methods can now be most effectively used? What part of the curriculum should be built around children's interests? What materials contribute best to the development of the individual children and what is the teacher's part in this new progress of education? First term. Credit, 2 semester hours.

Education S382. **Art As It Functions in the Primary Grades.** In the Progressive School art is one of the key subjects. This course is designed to give the classroom teacher practical help. First term. Credit, 2 semester hours.

Education S391. **Philosophies, Materials and Methods in the Intermediate Grades.** In this course problems similar to the following will be considered: In what way has education changed? What has brought about this change? What methods can now be most effectively used? What part of the curriculum should be built around children's interests? What materials contribute best to the development of the individual children and what is the teacher's part in this new progress of education? First term. Credit, 2 semester hours.

Education S392. **Art As It Functions in the Intermediate Grades.** In the Progressive School, art is one of the key subjects. This course is designed to give the classroom teacher practical help. First term. Credit, 2 semester hours.

Education S400. **Character Development.** This course is a study of the growth of character through school activities, both curricula and extra-curricula. Open to juniors and seniors. First term. Credit, 2 semester hours.

Education S401. **Present Day Educational Problems.** This course may be elected by students especially interested in research, who are approved by the instructor. Various modern problems will be taken up from a research angle. This will be of especial value to students who expect to do graduate work. First term. Credit, 2 semester hours.

Education S410. **Extra-Curricula Activities.** The following problems are among the more important studied in this course: school clubs, literary societies, dramatics, social functions, student participation in government, physical education, school publications, commencement, school lunch, national organizations such as boy scouts, girl scouts, etc. The training school is used as a laboratory for studying the practical application of many of these activities. The philosophy underlying an extra-curricula activity program is developed. Second term. Credit, 2 semester hours.

Education S420. **Vocational Guidance.** This course aims to introduce to the student the problems of educational and vocational guidance by a rapid survey of the literature in the field, and to set up standards for a comprehensive guidance program such as is feasible in the high schools of Alabama at the present time. The Alabama program for guidance through occupational studies for boys and girls is studied as one unit of the course. Other general topics studied are: vocational information and how the teacher may impart it, exploratory experiences as an essential feature of the junior high school program, vocational preparation, vocational counselling, and placement as a logical part of a comprehensive program of guidance. Open to juniors and seniors. Second term. Credit, 2 hours.

Education S440. **Directed Teaching in the Elementary Grades.** Required of all students who expect to apply for the College Elementary Class B Certificate. First term. Credit, 4 semester hours.

Education S450. **Directed Teaching in the High School.** Required of all students who are applicants for the College Secondary Class B Certificate. Students will not be permitted to teach subjects in which their college grade has been below "C". Directed teaching must be done in major and minor subjects. First term. Credit, to be arranged.

Education S460. **Tests and Measurements in Secondary Education.** This course is designed to give the student an understanding of the significance of modern testing procedures, and to furnish actual experience in administering tests and evaluating test results. Both old and new types of tests and examinations are studied, and the merits and demerits of each pointed out. Some time is spent on the theory of testing, including elementary statistical procedures and their application to classroom use. Some practice is given in the preparation of tests, as well as in giving tests and scoring papers. Open to seniors. First term. Credit, 2 semester hours.

Education S481. **Elementary School Administration.** This course will be open to a limited number of students who show special talent for this type of work. This will be of special value to prospective elementary school principals and supervisors. Prerequisite: Senior standing in the A.B. Elementary course. First term. Credit, 2 semester hours.

Education S490. **Principles of Education.** This course is a summarization of the problems of teaching. An objective will be the formulation of a definite philosophy of education by each student. Required of all students in the A.B. curriculum for secondary education. Second term. Credit, 2 semester hours.

ENGLISH

English S101. **Fundamentals of Composition.** Drill in the mechanics and practice in the fundamental forms of composition, both oral and written. Required in all curricula. First term. Credit, 3 semester hours.

English S102. **Forms of Composition.** A continuation of English S101. Reading in contemporary prose. Required in all curricula. First and second terms. Credit, 3 semester hours each term.

English S200. **Types of Poetry.** First and second terms. Credit, 3 semester hours each term.

English S320. **Survey of American Literature.** Study of the greater writers and their work viewed in the light of national and sectional conditions. Required in the A.B. Elementary curriculum. First and second terms. Credit, 2 or 3 semester hours each term.

English S350.2. **Teaching English in the High School.** Study of the special problems presented to the high school teacher of English. Materials and methods. Prerequisite: Sophomore English. First term. Credit, 2 or 3 semester hours.

English S360. **Writing for Publication.** A practice course in news and feature article writing. Prerequisite: 3 semester hours of Sophomore English. Second term. Credit, 2 or 3 semester hours.

English S472. **Contemporary Poetry.** Study of the chief British and American poets since 1890. A problem course. First term. Credit, 3 semester hours.

HISTORY

History S101. **History of Civilization.** History of civilization in the ancient period. For those students who have had less than one year of College History. First term. Credit, 3 semester hours.

History S102. **History of Civilization.** The history of civilization during the Middle Ages and the modern period. For those students who have had less than one year of College History. Second term. Credit, 3 semester hours.

History S201, S111. **History of the United States.** History of the United States through the colonial period and the organization of the government. Prerequisite: one year of History. First term. Credit, 3 semester hours.

History S202, S112. **History of the United States.** History of the United States from 1800 to 1914. Prerequisite: one year of History. Second term. Credit, 3 semester hours.

History S47I. **History of Alabama.** Recommended for History majors and minors and for juniors and seniors in the A.B. Elementary course. Second term. Credit, 3 semester hours.

Geography S203. **Geography of Europe.** This course deals with the economic, political, and social attitudes and activities of the European countries. First term. Credit, 2 semester hours.

Geography S231. **Survey of Geography.** Required of students taking the A.B. Elementary course. Open to all others who care to elect it. First term. Credit, 3 semester hours.

Political Science S302. **American Government.** A course for History majors and minors. Open to other juniors and seniors who care to take it. First term. Credit, 3 semester hours.

Economics 251 and Economics 350. **Elementary Economics.** Required of students majoring in Secretarial Science and Home Economics. Second term. Credit, 3 semester hours.

HOME ECONOMICS

The Family

Home Economics S400. **Child Growth and Development.** A study of the development, care, and training of the infant and pre-school child. Special emphasis will be given to the importance of home relationships. Undergraduate or graduate credit. Prerequisites: Psychology 250 or equivalent; Sociology 330; Home Economics 380, 350. (Home Economics majors). Fee $2.00. First term. Credit, 3 semester hours.

Home Economics S452. **Problems in Home and Family Life.** The practical application of the principles of sociology and economics to home and family life, emphasizing public health standards of living, house standards, household management, civic and social responsibilities. Undergraduate or graduate credit. Prerequisite: senior standing in home economics. Fee $2.00. First term. Credit, 2 semester hours.

The House and Its Administration

Home Economics S420. **Household Equipment.** Selection, care, and use; simple repairs. Undergraduate or graduate credit. Prerequisites: Physics 340, Home Economics 320. Fee $2.00. First term. Credit, 2 semester hours.

Home Economics S430. **Home Management.** The home situation as it is influenced by training. Study of consumption, use of leisure time and schedules. Undergraduate credit. Prerequisite: senior standing in home economics. First term. Credit, 2 semester hours.

Home Economics S500. **Seminar Economics of the Home.** A study of recent economic problems of the home as concerns equipment, cost of living, time and work studies. Graduate or registration approved. First term. Credit, 2 semester hours.

Clothing and Textiles

Home Economics S250. **Pattern Study and Garment Construction.** Comparison of line in commercial patterns; selection and durability of textile fabrics; original patterns developed from foundation pattern and used in the construction of a cotton or linen sport dress and a wool street dress; emphasis on designing and fitting. A project of a costume planned and constructed outside of class from the original pattern is required. Undergraduate credit. Prerequisite: Home Economics 102. Fee $2.00. First term. Credit, 3 semester hours.

Home Economics S352. **Textile Economics.** Study of the manufacture of familiar textile fibers and fabrics and its effect upon selection and durability. The economic and social significance of fashion and styling upon the merchandising of textiles and other commodities. Undergraduate or graduate credit. Prerequisite or parallel: Economics 350; Home Economics 350. Fee $2.00. First term. Credit, 3 semester hours.

Home Economics S550. **Clothing and Textile Seminar.** A study of recent clothing and textile investigations and research to acquaint students with latest developments in manufacture and consumption. Graduate or registration approved. First term. Credit, 1 semester hour.

Food and Nutrition

Home Economics S370. **Meal Study.** A study of menu planning for the family, stressing food selection and nutrition; organization of work; purchase and cost of food; meal preparation and table service. Undergraduate credit. Prerequisite: Home Economics 270; Chemistry 232. Fee $5.00. First term. Credit, 3 semester hours.

Home Economics S371. **Food Economics.** The study of market conditions and marketing; legislation pertaining to foodstuffs; food production and consumption; the purchasing of canned foods, package foods, staples, fresh fruits and vegetables, meats and dairy products as to quality, cost, use. Undergraduate or graduate credit. Fee $2.00. First term. Credit, 2 semester hours.

Home Economics S570. **Food Seminar.** A study of recent food investigations and research to acquaint students with latest developments in food preparation, production, and consumption. Graduate or registration approved. First term. Credit, 1 semester hour.

Home Economics Education

Home Economics S390. **Methods of Teaching Home Economics in High Schools.** A study of accepted educational principles applied to home economics teaching in high schools. Undergraduate credit. Prerequisite or parallel: Education 301; junior standing in Home Economics. First term. Credit, 3 semester hours.

Home Economics S492. **Vocational Education in Home Economics.** A study of the national and state programs for vocational education and their relation to the home economics program with special emphasis on the Alabama Vocational Home Economics program. Undergraduate credit. Prerequisite: Home Economics 490. First term. Credit, 3 semester hours.

Home Economics S590. **Seminar in Home Economics Education.** A study of recent educational studies and research to acquaint students with trends in education and home economics education. Graduate or registration approved. First term. Credit, 2 semester hours.

SCHOOL OF INSTRUCTION FOR VOCATIONAL HOME ECONOMICS TEACHERS

June 1—June 17, 1932

I.   **Introduction to Vocational Work.**

Study of the breadth of the program. State policies affecting the program. Organization problems, business management, promotion of the work in a community. One hour daily. Required of all teachers attending for the first time. Undergraduate credit, 1 semester hour.

II. **Methods of Teaching Home Economics.**

A study of accepted educational principles applied to home economics in high schools. One hour daily. Undergraduate credit, 1 semester hour.

III. **Management of Laboratory Classes.**

Organization of laboratory work, class room management, checking progress in laboratory classes. One hour daily. Undergraduate credit, 1 semester hour.

IV. **Home Economics with Out-of-School Groups.**

Promotion and organization of work with adults. Subject matter, methods, and devices to be used in such units. One hour daily. Undergraduate credit, 1 semester hour.

V.   **Home Improvement.**

Setting up objectives for such a program. Standards for the work. Informal landscaping, home beautification, improving health conditions. Two hours daily. Undergraduate credit, 1 semester hour.

VI. **Setting Up Objectives, Testing Progress, Grading.**

Setting up objectives for a lesson, or a problem, testing progress; using results of testing for further teaching, points to consider in grading. One hour daily. Undergraduate credit, 1 semester hour.

VII. **Home Projects and Joint Programs.**

Setting up objectives for such programs. Standards of work.

Types of projects, choosing projects, grading projects. Two hours daily. Undergraduate credit, 1 semester hour.

VIII. **A Program of Work.**

Points to consider, influencing factors, activities which may contribute to reaching the goals, setting up a specific program. One hour daily. Undergraduate and graduate credit, 1 semester hour.

IX. **The Ten Months Program.**

Opportunities and responsibilities of the ten months home economics program. One hour daily. Graduate credit, 1 semester hour.

X. **The Underlying Philosophy of a Home Economics Program.**

The purpose of educating youth, the contribution of home economics, the girl to be taught, determining objectives of home economics. One hour daily. Graduate credit, 1 semester hour.

XI. **Basic Principles of Learning.**

The desire to learn, the scientific attitude and method, developing thinking ways of learning. One hour daily. Graduate credit, 1 semester hour.

LIBRARY SCIENCE

Courses in Library Science for prospective Teacher-Librarians are open to juniors and seniors who are majoring in English, History, or Foreign Languages, and to graduates.

Library Science S301. **Book Selection.** A study of aids in selection and book evaluation. A minimum of fifteen books must be read and lists of books made, also a sample book order. Credit, 2 semester hours.

Library Science S320. **Administration and Organization.** A study of library standards, objectives, qualities of a librarian, and other phases of school library work. Visits will be made to libraries in. nearby cities. Credit, 2 semester hours.

Library Science S371. **Reference and Bibliography.** The study of more than a hundred standard reference books and special emphasis on those most used in schools. Credit, 2 semester hours.

Library Science S382. **Book Selection for Younger Children.** Emphasizes children's literature. Includes the reading of twenty books. Must be taken in connection with S301. Credit, 1 semester hour.

It is advised that those registering for Library Science during the summer take all the courses offered, for a Teacher-Librarian needs all of these.

MATHEMATICS

Mathematics S101. **College Algebra.** For students desiring college credit. Prerequisite: High School Algebra and Plane Geometry. First and second terms. Credit, 3 semester hours each term.

Mathematics S102. **Trigonometry.** For students desiring college credit. Prerequisite: High School Algebra and Plane Geometry. First and second terms.ᐧ Credit, 3 semester hours each term.

Mathematics S103. **College Algebra.** This course covers the more advanced portions of the subject, and is offered to meet the needs of those students who have completed part of the course in Algebra. Second term. Credit, 2 semester hours.

The first two courses are so arranged that students who have the approval of the Head of the Department of Mathematics may complete the full year's course in the summer school of eleven weeks.

MODERN LANGUAGE

French S101, S102. **Elementary French for College Students.** Grammar, composition, and reading of about one hundred pages of simple prose. Nine lesson periods a week. First and second terms. Credit, 3 semester hours each term.

French S201, S202. **Intermediate French.** Standard second year course, with a review of grammar, intermediate composition and reading of about three hundred pages of fairly difficult French prose. Nine lesson periods a week. First and second terms. Credit, 3 semester hours each term.

German S101, S102. **Elementary German.** A college course for beginners. Grammar and reading texts will be used to lay the foundation for reading, writing, and speaking German. Nine lesson periods a week. First and second terms. Credit, 3 semester hours each term.

Spanish S101, S102. **Elementary Spanish for Beginners.** The scope of the course embraces the elements of grammar, correct pronunciation, simple conversation and reading of easy prose. Nine lesson periods a week. First and second terms. Credit, 3 semester hours each term.

Spanish S201, S202. **Intermediate Spanish.** Standard second year course, with a rapid review of grammar, more advanced work in syntax, writing of short essays, and reading of representative works of modern authors. Nine lesson periods a week. First and second terms. Credit, 3 semester hours each term.

Note: Students who attend both terms of the Alabama College Summer School may complete a year of work in a modern language.

MUSIC*

The music work during the summer session aims to serve several widely divergent fields of music. As in the past the field of performance in organ, piano, violin, and voice will be ably presented. The courses will be organized upon a slightly different basis than formerly. Public School Music Methods will be offered as usual. The School has added to its equipment of orchestral instruments and is now able to offer full work in Wind and String Pedagogy. Music Education at the Piano, the application of psychology to the problems of education for musicianship through piano study, will be offered for teachers. Those who are preparing for the state certificate examination will find work organized for their need.

APPLIED MUSIC

Repertory Classes

The courses in Applied Music are divided into two types. One group of courses serves those who are already established musicians, who wish to add to their repertory or to re-study and re-interpret familiar works. To permit full consideration of more extended compositions two one-hour lessons a week are assigned to this group of courses. The lessons are private. It will be possible to register for part of the course in case one cannot remain for the entire six weeks. Registration for the Repertory Classes includes registration in the Lecture Class in Piano. These lecture-recitals will be given once each week by Mr. Ziolkowski. The Ensemble Class may be substituted by students of violin.

The second group of Applied Music courses will meet the needs of the student who is approaching the study of the literature of the instrument for the first time and who is still working for the formation of an adequate technic. These courses will also serve those who do not wish to devote themselves exclusively to the study of an instrument. These courses may also be taken for less than the full credit. The Lecture Class in Piano or the Ensemble Class is also open to registrants in this course with special permission of the instructor.

The work in the above mentioned courses will be offered by:

Organ: Colin B. Richmond
       Harrison D. LeBaron
Piano: Miecislaw Ziolkowski
Violin: Ronald Ingalls
Voice: Katherine Farrah

Public School Music

This summer an effort is made to present more fully than formerly the material for the establishing of school orchestras and bands. The

---

*The courses indicated under this heading are offered in the first term of the summer school. Those interested in music study during the second term should consult with the Director of the School of Music before July 1.

School is now equipped with the essential instruments so that the student may become conversant with the needs of the player of any of the important band and orchestral instruments. A course in instrumental and choral conducting is also offered for the benefit of the beginner in this field.

The Applied Music study of students in this field may be done with one lesson a week if desired. If numbers warrant, lessons in orchestral instruments may be offered as a combination of one private and one class lesson.

The usual courses in Public School Music will be offered.

Work in this field will be offered by:

Methods: . . . . Mary Zielinski
Band and Orchestral Pedagogy: Ronald Ingalls
Mary Zielinski

Music Education at the Piano

This course, designed for teachers of piano, will consider primarily the needs of the pupil. The aim of the course will be a thorough understanding of the aims of musical education rather than a memorizing of any particular set of devices seeking hazily understood objectives. A thorough study will be made of the underlying psychology of musical listening and performance. The possible aims for listening and performance will be considered, and a philosophy of musicianship built. The application of these principles to the mental processes of the student will be studied, together with the development of proper attitudes. In addition to the theoretical discussions, the course will form itself into a group of class piano where concrete examples of the building of musicianship will be sought.

Those intending to take the state examination for a certificate will find this work helpful. This course will be offered by Harrison D. LeBaron.

Theory

The Theory courses offered carry the work from beginning Harmony through Composition. As far as possible the work under this heading will be directed to meet the immediate needs of the student. Work in courses not outlined may be pursued if it is possible to arrange the instruction.

Music Fees

The fees listed below include the fee for practice and the credit hour fee: that is, the total expense of a course is indicated here.

Applied Music:

12 private hour lessons and
12 lecture or ensemble classes _____ _____$35.00
12 private half-hour lessons _____ ____ 24.00
Music Education at the Piano _____ 18.00
Harmony _____ 6.00

Solfeggio _____ 3.00
Analysis _____ 6.00
Liturgical Music _____ 3.00
Composition _____ 6.00
School Music Methods _____ 6.00
Instrumental Pedagogy _____ 6.00
Conducting _____ 3.00

Description of Courses

Music S103. **Music Education at the Piano.** As far as practical this course will be conducted by the discussion method. Class work in piano, the evolution of music history, psychology of music, aesthetics, musical form. Five double periods a week of recitation. First term. Credit, 4 semester hours.

Music S101. **Harmony.** Primary triads and their inversions, cadences, the dominant seventh chords and their inversions. Text: Chadwick—Harmony. Prerequisite: Music S90. First term. Credit, 3 semester hours.

Music S102. **Harmony.** Secondary chords and inversions, dominant ninth and its inversions, diminished sevenths and their inversions, modulation, etc. Text: Chadwick—Harmony. Prerequisites: Music S90 and S101. First term. Credit, 3 semester hours.

Music S101. **Solfeggio and Dictation.** Drill in scale and interval singing, part singing, elementary rhythmic problems, dictation to train the ear to recognize intervals, common triads, etc. Text: Ear-Training and Sight-Singing, Wedge. First term. Credit, 1 semester hour.

Music S103. **Choir Conducting and Liturgical Music.** This course is designed primarily for music teachers who are interested in organ work and who do choir training. This is a lecture course for the most part, with some demonstration work. It is an advanced course in choir management and music of the Church. First term. Credit, 1 semester hour.

Music S301. **Structural Analysis.** Homophonic and contrapuntal forms together with a consideration of the structural detail of composition. Prerequisite: a course in Harmony. First term. Credit, 2 semester hours.

Music S302. **Harmonic Analysis.** Analytical study of the harmony of Wagner, Franck, and a contemporary composer. Prerequisite: a course in Harmony. First term. Credit, 2 semester hours.

Music S301. **Composition.** Vocal writing. Short solo and choral settings. Instrumental three part song form. Permission of the instructor required for admission. First term. Credit, 2 semester hours.

Music S103. **Public School Music.** Drill in scale and interval singing, part singing, elementary rhythmic problems, dictation to train the ear to recognize intervals, common triads, etc., with two additional hours of choral rehearsal. First term. Credit, 1 semester hour.

Music S301: **Public School Music Methods for Primary and Inter-mediate Grades.** Study of the methods of presenting music in first six grades according to the class methods employed in public schools; selection and presentation of rote songs; care of child voice; introduction of staff notation; presentation of tonal and rhythmic problems of each grade; lessons in directed listening; more recent practices in creative music for children; beginning of instrumental instruction; methods of utilizing radio in music education; survey of educational school broadcasts; readings and reports of contemporary thought on school music problems. Theory and practice of teaching combined in class work. Five hours a week. First term. Credit, 2 semester hours.

Music S401. **Public School Music Methods for Junior and Senior High Schools.** Study of the adolescent voice, its care; testing and classifying voices; selection of materials; organization of bands and orchestras; class instrumental teaching; public performances; school assembly; class voice teaching; music appreciation materials; project method of music instruction; newer movements in high school music education. Application of methods of teaching by practical work with the class itself. Readings and reports on contemporary thought on high school music problems. Five hours a week. First term. Credit, 2 semester hours.

Music S201. **Public School Music Appreciation.** Methods of presenting this subject to children; evaluation of courses of study in music appreciation. Bibliography of available texts on appreciation for children is made. Three hours a week. First term. Credit, 1 semester hour.

Music S301. **Wind Instrument Pedagogy.** Brass and wood wind instruments. A preparation for conducting school orchestras and bands; procedure for class teaching, principles of holding, fingering and playing the different instruments. The student gets practical experience in playing on instruments of each type. Students should bring their own instruments when possible. Two double periods a week. First term. Credit, 2 semester hours.

Music S401. **String Instrument Pedagogy.** A preparation for conducting school orchestras; procedure for class teaching; survey of materials for class teaching; principles of holding, fingering, and playing instruments. Practical experience in playing on instruments of each type. The students should bring their own instruments when possible. Two double periods a week. First term. Credit, 2 semester hours.

Music S301. **Conducting.** A study of the principles underlying ensemble performance. Practice in the use of the baton; a study of interpretation and its indication. First term. Credit, 1 semester hour.

PHYSICAL EDUCATION

Physical Education S152. **Beginning Swimming.** First and second terms. Credit, 1 semester hour each term.

Physical Education S200. **General Activities.** This course includes games, stunts, clogging, and folk dancing. First term. Credit, 1 semester hour.

Physical Education S252. **Intermediate Swimming.** First and second terms. Credit, 1 semester hour each term.

Physical Education S272. **Rural Community and School Hygiene.** Problems and methods of teaching hygiene in the grades, including posture tests and health campaigns. First term. Credit, 2 semester hours.

Physical Education S352. **Life Saving.** First and second terms. Credit, 1 semester hour each term.

Physical Education S360.7. **Physical Education for Elementary Schools.** A survey of the state course of study for the elementary schools with special emphasis on material, organization, and methods. First term. Credit, 3 semester hours.

Physical Education S361. **Coaching.** This course includes the coaching of Basket-ball, Baseball, and Volley-ball. First term. Credit, 2 semester hours.

Physical Education S370.7. **Physical, Education for High Schools.** A study of the state point system for high school girls with emphasis on material, organization, record keeping and methods. First term. Credit, 3 semester hours.

PSYCHOLOGY

Psychology S201. **General Psychology.** Innate and acquired factors in behavior; motivation of behavior; individual differences and their measurement; problems of learning; personality adjustments. Scientific method illustrated with simple experiments which form the basis of teaching. Required of A. B. Liberal Arts and Secondary Education students and also of students majoring in Sociology and Physical Education. First term. Credit, 3 semester hours.

Psychology S202. **General Psychology.** A continuation of Psychology S201. Second term. Credit, 3 semester hours.

Psychology S300. **Educational Psychology.** This course includes a study of the laws of learning, reasoning and imagining, transfer of training, factors influencing efficiency, individual differences in intelligence, achievement and capacity. Required of A. B. Elementary and A. B. Secondary students, also of Secretarial students. Prerequisite: Psychology 251 or 152 or equivalent. First and second terms. Credit, 3 semester hours each term.

Psychology S500. **Psychology of Adolescence.** The course treats of general methods of child study as related to the adolescent in particular. It includes studies of adolescent interests, abilities and personality. Social and educational adjustment problems are discussed as well as problems of mental hygiene, vocational guidance and personality development. Prerequisite: five hours of General Psychology or the equivalent. First term. Graduate credit. Credit, 3 semester hours.

RELIGIOUS EDUCATION

Religious Education S201. **The Acts of the Apostles.** This is primarily a historical study of the early Christian Church beginning with the Ascension of Christ and continuing through the active service of the Apostle Paul. We have in this story, therefore, the founding, broadening and extension of the Christian Church in the world. Open to all students. First term. Credit, 2 semester hours.

Religious Education S401. **The Curriculum of Religious Education.** This course will provide the student with a general survey of the modern conception of the aims and purposes of religious education today. It should be especially helpful to all of those who are active in the Church's educational program and who desire to become more efficient in that phase of their work. Open to all students. First term. Credit, 2 semester hours.

Religious Education S402. **Religious Education in the Family.** This course should be especially attractive to teachers who are interested in offering helpful suggestions to parents relative to their responsibility for the religious development of their children in the home. A mastery of the materials offered will add tremendously to the teacher's ability to deal with certain problems growing out of maladjustment in the home. Open to all students. First term. Credit, 2 semester hours.

SECRETARIAL

Typewriting S101. **Fundamentals of Touch Writing.** Operation of the machine; the keyboard; straight copy; and simple letter arrangement. First term. Credit, 3 semester hours.

SOCIOLOGY

Sociology S201. **Introductory Sociology.** This course is designed to serve as a preliminary survey for those who plan to continue further in the field of sociology, and at the same time to provide students majoring in other fields with some insight into human origins and institutions. A background for clear thinking regarding social processes and social problems is given in an analysis of the primary factors in social life—the geographical, the biological, the psychological, and the cultural. First term. Credit, 3 semester hours.

Sociology S202. **Introductory Sociology.** A continuation of Sociology S201. Upon the basis of the primary factors of social life, there is a study of certain fundamental social arrangements whereby man has solved the major problems of living together in groups; material culture; myth, magic, religion and science; the family and its problems; and the State. Second term. Credit, 3 semester hours.

Sociology S210. **Principles of Sociology.** This course, designed for the student majoring in other fields, aims to analyze and interpret social experience and thus prepare the student for a more intelligent participation in social life. A study is made of the origin of social experience and the nature of personality and of the organization of human experience into social institutions—the family, property, the state, the church. First term. Credit, 2 semester hours.

Sociology S220. **An Introduction to the Study of Rural Sociology.** A survey of the physical, economic and social aspects of farm life. Special emphasis upon the major problems growing out of rural living. Required of majors in Home Economics. First and second terms. Credit, 3 semester hours.

Sociology S321. **Principles of Case Work.** A course intended for professional students. It deals with the general principles of social treatment of families in need. The course is based upon the study of case records and a systematic consideration of (1) the problems growing out of sickness, insanity or feeble-mindedness, non-residence, death, accident or desertion of child bread winner, old age, illegitimacy, and dependency, and (2) the technique employed in meeting these problems. First term. Credit, 3 semester hours each term.

Sociology S330. **Family Relations.** Brief sketch of the history of the family; the home; family relations. First term. Credit, 3 semester hours.

Sociology S340. **Recreational Leadership.** A study of special movements and new theory and practice in recreational organizations, planning, and leadership. This course offers practical instruction and field work. First term. Credit, 3 semester hours.

Sociology S370. **Field Work in Social Service.** A course offering practical experience for professional students in the field of rural social work. Arrangements are made for the students to work twelve to fifteen hours a week with the Shelby County Child Welfare Department as probation officers, school attendance officers, family welfare workers. The field work is carried on under the joint supervision of a member of the college faculty and the County Superintendent· of Child Welfare. First term. Credit, 3 semester hours.

Sociology S380. **Social Ethics.** Personal and social morality; a critical evaluation of the methods employed by society in handling the criminal, the immigrant, the poor; the race problems. Second term. Credit, 2 semester hours.

SPEECH

The work of this department is two-fold; personal development and professional training. The personal development work aims to correct the most salient defects in voice and body, thus making the personality more effective. The professional training covers the field of interpretation which is divided into public speaking, public reading and dramatic art. The student thus prepared is equipped to teach the various phases of expression work, and coach plays and contests in school or community, as well as to entertain.

Speech S101. **Principles of Speech.** A fundamental course in general speech education. Training embraces the development of voice and action applied in oral discourse; breath control; voice placement, resonance, phrasing, emphasis, platform manner. First term. Credit, 3 semester hours.

Speech S131. **Principles.** A fundamental course designed to give speech training to those who need the work but cannot give the time S101 requires. First term. Credit, 1 semester hour.

Speech S141. **Story Telling.** Study of child psychology, leading to consideration of stories suitable for children. Principles and aim. Practice in class and story hour groups in telling of stories for schools and centers. First term. Credit, 2 semester hours.

Speech S300. **Play.** A summer school play will be produced. Anyone enrolled in summer school is eligible to try out. Those selected for the cast will receive credit. First term. Credit, 1 semester hour.

Speech S381. **Auditorium.** This course is designed to meet the needs of the auditorium teacher. It is a study of the way schools have used the hour and includes helps, suggestions, and bibliography for practical application. First term. Credit, 2 semester hours.

Speech S400. **Play Production.** An intensive general course designed to aid teachers hitherto not fully prepared who find themselves confronted with the problem of production. It will include such problems as choosing, casting and staging a play, as well as the direction. First term. Credit, 2 semester hours.

In case the above courses do not develop, the following may be offered:

Speech S111 or S112. **Acting.** Principles of dramatic work. Character development. Preparation for presentation in public production. First term. Credit, 2 semester hours.

Speech S211, S212, S311, S312. **Advanced Acting.** First term. Credit, 1 or 2 semester hours.

Speech, private lessons. Personal attention to the application of principles in platform reading; development in interpretative ability. Hours and credits arranged. Special fee.

*HIGH SCHOOL SUBJECTS
First Term
Senior High School

English S3a. **Composition and Literature.** Standard Senior II High School English. Texts: Baker and Goddard, English Fundamentals; Woolley, New Handbook of Composition; Greenlaw and Others, Literature and Life, Book III. Credit, ½ unit.

English S4a. **Composition and Literature.** Standard Senior III High School English. Texts: Woolley, New Handbook of Composition; Greenlaw and Others, Literature and Life, Book IV. Credit, ½ unit.

History S3a. **American History.** Standard Senior II High School History. Text: Mace, American History. Credit, ½ unit.

History S4a. **Citizenship.** Standard Senior III High School History. Text: Hughes, Problems of American Democracy. Credit, ½ unit.

Mathematics S3a. **Plane Geometry.** A study of the first two books. Text: Newell and Harper, Plane Geometry. Credit, ½ unit.

Mathematics S4a. **Algebra.** Prerequisite; one unit of high school Algebra or its equivalent. Text: Wells and Hart, Modern Second Course in Algebra. Credit, ½ unit.

SECOND TERM

English S3b. A continuation of English S3a. Credit, ½ unit.

English S4b. A continuation of English S4a. Credit, ½ unit.

History S3b. A continuation of History S3a. Credit, ½ unit.

History S4b. A continuation of History S4a. Credit, ½ unit.

Mathematics S3b. **Plane Geometry.** A continuation of Mathematics S3a offered the first term. Plane Geometry, Books III, IV, and V. Text: Same as first term. Credit, ½ unit.

Mathematics S4b. **Solid Geometry.** This course is for students desiring high school credit. Students who have not had this subject and who wish to major in mathematics in college are advised to take it. Text: Newell and Harper, Solid Geometry. Credit, ½ unit.

*All high school classes will meet twice daily.

THE THIRTY-SEVENTH ANNUAL SESSION OF ALABAMA COLLEGE OPENS SEPTEMBER 5, 1932

The college is a member of the Association of Alabama Colleges, the Association of Colleges and Secondary Schools of the Southern States, and of the Association of American Colleges.

In its efforts to meet the needs of the young women in the State, Alabama College offers the following curricula:

FOUR-YEAR CURRICULA

Curricula leading to the Bachelor of Arts Degree in the liberal art subjects, preparation for teaching in high school, and preparation for teaching in the elementary school.

Curricula leading to the Bachelor of Science Degree in Art, Biology, Biology and Chemistry, Chemistry, Home Economics, Physical Education, Secretarial Science, and Social Service and Attendance Work.

Curricula leading to the Bachelor of Music Degree in Piano, Organ, Violin, Voice, and Public School Music.

The college offers excellent accommodations at reasonable rates for the number of students that will be accepted.

For the regular catalog and further information address

ALABAMA COLLEGE
MONTEVALLO, ALABAMA

APPLICATION FOR ADMISSION

to

ALABAMA COLLEGE SUMMER SCHOOL

Montevallo, Alabama

SUMMER SESSION—1932

Date_____

1. Name (in full) _____

2. Address: Street and No., or R. F. D. _____

   City _____, County _____, State _____ ___

3. Name and address of parent or guardian _____

4. Last school attended _____

   Graduate? _____

5. Enclosed is reservation fee of $2.00. Please (reserve) (do not reserve) a place in the college dormitory for me. (Strike out word or words in parentheses.)

6. If you want an Identification Certificate for **Reduced Railroad** Rates, check here_____. They will be mailed out to those desiring them a short time before the date for purchasing tickets (See page 19.) If you fail to receive yours, one will be sent to you on request.

7. Indicate courses desired:

   _____

   _____

   _____

   _____

   _____

   Remarks _____

   Signature of Applicant _____

CPSIA information can be obtained
at www.ICGtesting.com
Printed in the USA
BVHW041725051118
532208BV00024B/4720/P